BETWEEN
WEBSTER
&ME

Carol Joan Campbell

Inks and Bindings
888-290-5218
www.inksandbindings.com
orders@inksandbindings.com

Dedication [ˌdediˈkā SH ən]

Dedicated to my husband, Bill, and my children, Bruce, Laurie, and Brent, who have shown me the true meaning of love: "1. deep and tender feelings of affection; encourage: 2. to give support to; be favorable to; foster; help; and patience: 1a. the will or ability to wait or endure without complaint."

Author's Note

As you read the following pages, please note that all of the words that are enclosed in quotation marks are actual definitions taken from *Webster's New World Dictionary of the American Language-Second College Edition,* published by Simon and Schuster. I truly hope that you will enjoy this book as much as I enjoyed writing it—then we'll both be winners. I found it to be a challenge that was both informational and educational. I found words new to me and familiar words that had unexpected definitions that delighted and confounded me. Actually reading a dictionary was a new experience. Please be warned that I became rather addicted to it, so plan on seeing the next book soon.

Just Who Is Webster Anyhow?

Noah Webster was born on October 16, 1758. His family lived in West Hartford, Connecticut. Noah had two brothers and two sisters. Noah's father was a farmer and weaver ("Webster" comes from Old English and means "female weaver"). His mother, Mercy, was a homemaker.

Most kids at that time only went to school until they were ten or eleven. After that, they stayed home to work on the farm. But when Noah was fourteen, he began studying with a minister. After two years, he went to Yale College and graduated in 1778. He wanted to study to be a lawyer but didn't have enough money. Instead of studying law, Noah became a schoolmaster in Hartford, Litchfield, and Sharon, all in Connecticut.

Teachers in the late 1700s taught all grades together in one room. One teacher might have children from ages six to sixteen. The books were not well written and were published in England. Schools had bad lighting and not enough heat in the winter. Based on his experiences, Noah wrote essays about improving the poor conditions for teachers and students. During this time, he kept reading and studying law. He was admitted to the bar (an association for lawyers) and received his Master of Arts degree in 1781.

One cause Noah believed passionately in was that American children should have American textbooks. In 1783 he finished *A Grammatical Institute of the English Language*. It included *The Blue-backed Speller*, a textbook that helped kids learn to read, spell, and pronounce words.

Building on his earlier passions for education reform and his education in law, Noah became a political journalist, writing pamphlets such as "The Effects of Slavery on Morals and Industry" (1793), "The Revolution in France" (1794), and, "The Rights of Neutral Nations" (1802). He traveled to many places, selling his *Sketches of American Policy*, written in 1785.

Noah was married in 1789 and practiced law in Hartford for four years before returning to New York City, where he worked on the city's first daily newspaper, *The American Minerva* (1793—1798). His primary passion, however, was words.

In 1798, he moved to New Haven. Noah also served in the Connecticut House of Representatives in 1800 and 1802 through 1807, and as a county judge in 1807. Noah realized that people in the United States were using different words to describe their new government and laws, which prompted his decision to write an American dictionary. In 1806, he published a shortened version. It had 40, 600 words. Twenty-two years later, the final version was published. *An American Dictionary of the English Language (1828)* had about seventy thousand words and definitions. Webster included spelling, pronunciation, and information about the history of each word.

It is not so widely known that around this time Noah produced his own modern English translation of the Bible, which was published in 1833. It wasn't widely accepted, due to the popularity of the traditional King James Version, but was the most significant English language translation of the Scriptures to be done since the King James Version of more than two hundred years earlier.

A second edition of his dictionary, "corrected and enlarged," was published in 1841. It became known popularly as *Webster's Unabridged.* He completed the revision of an appendix of this edition a few days before his death, which occurred in New Haven on the twenty-eighth of May 1843.

It took him a long time to compile the dictionary, as it required a lot of research. Most of the words we use today come from other languages, such as Latin or French. Noah learned twenty-six languages so that he could figure out the origins of our words.

After Noah Webster died, a publishing company called G. & C. Merriam Co. bought all the unsold copies of the 1841 edition of Webster's dictionary. They also bought from his family the rights to update and sell new versions of the dictionary. Today, *Merriam-Webster's Collegiate Dictionary* has more than 225,000 definitions—more than three times as many as Webster's original book.

Webster's dictionary was so popular that "Webster's" became synonymous with dictionary to many Americans. As a result, the Webster's name lost trademark protection and is now used by numerous publishers in the titles of their dictionaries. Among these, the Merriam-Webster's dictionary is considered to be the most direct descendent of Noah Webster's lexicographical tradition, the Merriam brothers having purchased the rights to revise the dictionary from Webster's heirs upon his death.

Oh yes, one more thing. Noah began laying the foundation for copyright laws. He thought America should have laws to protect the words of its authors. In 1790, the first federal, or national, copyright law was passed. It protected an original piece of work from being copied for fourteen years after it was created.

Therefore, if you wish to copy any of the information in this book, sorry. You'll have to wait for a few years.

Appeal [əˈpēl]

While going through the pages of the dictionary, I wondered what word would appeal to me to begin my journey *Between Webster and Me.* Being a little slow on the take, it took me a few more pages before discovering that I had already chosen a start—*Appeal.* Actually, that sounded very appealing.

This is a word that is commonly used, whether spoken, heard, or read. It really has a nice sound to it. Sort of rolls off your tongue in a soft way. Hard to make it come across as harsh. I actually did try!

It would be great to hear someone tell me how appealing my book will be. It is nice to hear how appealing the scent of my perfume is or how appealing the house smells when bread is baking. (Yes, I still make bread!)

Most people desire to know that they appeal to others. That means, of course, that others like us, a good feeling. What qualities do we have to have to be appealing? Aha— that seems to depend upon who is looking at us.

In the area of love, a male/female finds another person appealing. Be it by the looks of the other person, the wit they display, their interesting conversations, the way they dress—or any of a number of oh so many other directions. Perhaps this appeal may turn to love, but probably at least a desire to get to know someone better.

Of course I can't help but mention sex appeal. Just watch television any day or night. Go to most of the newest movies that appear on the big screen in theatres. Most every star that makes it big isn't always judged by how well they read their lines, but how sexy all of their lines (or curves) look. Dress designers seem to follow those directions also.

I'll go back to Webster now and see what he says. "To appeal is to be attractive, interesting; arouse a favorable response." Certainly that covers it well. Why not love a person who has those qualifications?

Watch out for the next step, however. *Webster's* also defines this word to mean an "urgent request to a person for help, sympathy, etc." Sounds to me like you had better evaluate this person Whom you now think is wonderful to see if you are ready to take on any burdens that they are ready to place on you. I'm not sure now if I really want to come across appealing to everyone.

Here's the same word applied to law: "The transference of a case to a higher Court for rehearing or review." Suddenly this word has changed from a complimentary, endearing application into a deep legal quandary. Luckily *Webster's* calls upon a higher court in a synonym application and makes things right with the word and with the world by turning *appeal* toward religious application. "To supplicate and pray, suggesting humility in entreaty and imply the request is made to God or to a superior authority—supplicate in addition suggesting a kneeling or other abjectly prayerful attitude."

I fully understand this word now, and I'm ready to forge forward into seeking more words, sure that I will find this whole process not just informative, but most appealing.

Buffet [bəˈfət]

Here's one word that all of us automatically know and enjoy. Most of us are really happy when we go to a restaurant and see on the menu that they offer a buffet—be it for breakfast, lunch, or dinner. This opens up a wonderful chance for making our own choices of food, amounts that we want to take, and an opportunity to stuff ourselves.

It also conjures up visions of epic movies where kings and their courts were seated at long tables covered with every sort of food that was available at that time. It was all set before them, and everyone dug in. Uninhibited by knives and forks, they simply used their personal utensils—hands, fingers, teeth—ripping the meat apart, letting the juices drip where they may, pulling off chunks of bread, grabbing at anything that looked pleasing to them. Finally to finish there were apples, bunches of grapes, berries, and who knows what all that they were able to harvest. Of course, by this time, the beautiful girls were dancing, the jester was trying to keep everyone awake, and who cared if they did fall asleep? Their stomachs were full and, therefore, content.

Now, I'll return to the present time. We have a larger variety of food available at our buffets than anyone could have imagined in those olden days. We happily go to get our plates and begin filling them. Of course, mothers are usually reminding everyone, "Now don't take more than you think you can eat." Okay, that's fine; after all, we can always go back for a second helping, or a third for that matter.

So, we get back to our table to eat. Now, of course, we have to contend with knives, forks, spoons, and napkins. Don't take such big bites; chew your food carefully before you put more in your mouth. Don't talk with your mouth full. Certainly we have to eat properly, remembering to dab our mouths occasionally so we look neat at all times.

Next there's that word that seems to be on everyone's minds this day and age—calories. If one has some of this, one probably shouldn't take some of that. Then you have to make trade offs, and if you want to truly enjoy at least one or two of those sumptuous desserts at the end, you'd better not go back for those seconds after all.

Oh well, at least we know about buffets. Okay, Webster, what else is there to know? What? Where's the beef? A buffet is what?

"1. A piece of furniture with drawers and cupboards for dishes, table linen, silver, etc.; 2. A counter or table where refreshments are served; and finally, 3. A meal at which guests serve themselves from a buffet or table.

Guess we all concentrate on eating and not what the food sits on. Okay, there's one more meaning, spelled the same, but pronounced a bit differently: "A blow with the hand or fist; to punch or slap."

Perhaps that's *Webster's* reminder to put the right emphasis on the right syllable. Ba fay': eating lots of food. Buf'it: what you're liable to get if you try and grab too much food.

Circle [ˈsərkəl]

When you look at a circle on paper, Webster's first definition is easy to understand, "1. A plain figure bounded by a single curved line every point of which is equally distant from the point at the center of the figure. "

Going one step further, however, was not that easy. After several attempts to draw a circle, it was an accomplishment just to have the ends meet. In desperation, I rummaged through my desk to find my old school supplies (of course these are *really* old now), and came upon my ruler, protractor, and compass. No, not the compass you carry when you're out walking so that you can hopefully find your way back to your original starting point, but a contraption that has two legs. One leg has a place where a pencil can be inserted, and the other has a sharp point on it. You open the two legs to whatever size you want the circle to be. Then you tighten it, insert the point, and slowly press the pencil around on the paper, and you have a circle. Yay!

When finally succeeding in drawing a circle that looked really good, I had now formed "2. The circumference." I vaguely remember my math teacher of high school days pounding on the formula for calculating the answer to the circumference of a circle.

While we are on the topic of mathematical equations, keep in mind that a circle is a zero, which equals nothing, so probably not even worth mentioning.

Webster must have kept going around in circles just trying to define the word, and started the list as follows, "3. Anything shaped like a circle, a ring, crown, halo, etc."

Here are some more familiar things: drinking glasses, cereal bowls, saucepans, frying pans—that's just in the kitchen—hats, bracelets, and, of course, rings. Yes, of course, they have to be round to fit on fingers, but let's think of the lovely connotation suggested at weddings: an unending circle of love to remind couples of their devotion to one another.

Another definition, which has always been a wonder to me and to astrologists, "5. The orbit of a heavenly body." With more knowledge of outer space and space shuttles, etc., most of us are truly aware of how the planets circle the earth and the pictures relayed via movies and TV showing earth as just a small circle in space.

Speaking of outer space, can't help but remember when we were on a plane coming back from a vacation when lots of flights were coming into the airport. The pilot informed us that we would have to circle the airport for a while because of congested landing arrivals. Of course we don't know if he formed perfect circles around each time, but I do remember that my head was practically spinning in circles by the time we finally got our turn to land. For a few weeks after that, every time we gathered with our various circles of friends, "8. A group of people bound together by common interests", they were destined to hear the tale about how many miles we traveled in a circle while waiting to land.

Delicate [ˈdelikit]

What a lovely word. It sort of tickles your tongue to even say it. No matter how hard you try, it just can't be said angrily. No, it's sweet, gentle, and beautiful.

Images appear in my mind when hearing this word. My impressions seem light, airy, the features of a beautiful child's face. The gorgeous piece of lace that was a part of your wedding gown. The tiny figure made of porcelain that sits on a high shelf to keep it safely out of reach from small hands that could harm it in any way. Touching a small baby ever so lightly just to feel the softness of his skin. This word seems to conjure up dreams, memories, and love. Could there be anything that isn't wonderful about this word?

Okay, time to check *Webster's*. On this one, we fully agree: "1. pleasing in its lightness, mildness, subtlety; beautifully fine in texture, quality, workmanship, etc." Well, he does go in another direction—perhaps hinted at in my first paragraph: "4. easily damaged, spoiled, disordered, needing special handling." That's easy to understand, as we want to preserve the beauty of all of our delicate possessions; so naturally we're going to be very cautious about how they are taken care of.

I'm sure we have all known some dear person in our lives who was in poor health and was considered to be very delicate. I now envision the tiny, little lady we saw in a wheel chair at the nursing home when we went there to visit our friend. She looked so fragile, but, of course, still beautiful. As we came nearer to her, we could even see more closely the delicate shade of lavender in the shawl around her tiny shoulders, knitted in a delicate lace pattern. When we took the time to sit close to her, we even noticed the delicate aroma of her rose water cologne and saw her beautiful smile that lit up her delicate features. This was perhaps a delicate situation, as we didn't really know this person, but when she smiled, we became "7. finely sensitive in feeling, understanding and responding." We, indeed, turned a delicate ear toward her quiet conversation, and we too responded in a soft, delicate manner. Yes, it was a lovely time.

Always keep this word close in your thoughts and in your heart. Every precious thing we have should always be handled in a delicate way. Also, every precious person we know needs to be shown "tact, understanding, and sensitive consideration" so their perhaps delicate feelings will never be hurt or offended by us.

Elute [iˈloōt] and Elutriate [iˈloōtrē͵āt]

This one was a real stickler. Don't ever remember hearing anyone utter these words. I never remember even seeing them on the printed pages of any books along the way. With the exception of *Webster's* big book, that is. Let's analyze. Perhaps a derivative of elite? Elude?

No, neither of those words made any sense to me. I actually contemplated just turning more pages, ignoring the puzzle. However, my goal in searching the dictionary was to discover words that had to be researched a bit and look for clues in the definitions.

When you spill paint, you may use this. If you eat in a sloppy manner, you will probably do this to your shirt or blouse afterward.

The next one was easy, as most people do this every morning. Many times we do this to fresh vegetables or wild rice. We also do this when we serve canned vegetables.

This intense concentrating was becoming rather tiresome. The search other examples had become fruitless.

Suddenly, in a moment of inspiration, my brain kicked in and gave me a brilliant idea. I'll just take the complete definition from the pages of *Webster's*.

Elute: "To wash out; to remove (adsorbed material) by use of a solvent." Elutriate: "To wash out, rack off. To wash. To purify by washing and straining or by decanting."

Oh no, Noah has done it again—used a word in a definition that needed to be looked up before completely understanding the full definition. I took a deep breath and turned back to look up decanting. *Decanting* means "to pour off a liquid gently, or to pour from one container to another."

I did my duty and found a new word to use, and I'll probably worry anyone who is a guest at my dinner table when I excuse myself to take care of decanting the vegetables and elutriating my hands.

Face [fās]

This seems like such a simple word. When you look into a mirror, you'll see your face. We meet another person, and we see their face. It simply means "1. the front of the head, from the top of the forehead to the bottom of the chin, and from ear to ear." It is easy for children to know the faces of their moms and dads and all of their friends. Okay, no real explanation needed.

While still thinking of this word, I had to run over to the mall and pick up something. After shopping for a while, I stopped at a snack bar to have a coke and couldn't help but smile while watching a little boy sitting with his dad and making terrible faces (the boy, that is, not the dad). Predictably, the dad of this young lad was getting annoyed and told him he better quit making faces or he would end up looking like that all the time.

Of course I had my pocket-sized dictionary with me, and it was obvious that Webster had seen similar behavior with kids in his time when he came up with this meaning:

"to distort the face in a way, expressing anger, contempt, or distaste."

The English language is not simple, I'm afraid. Webster certainly recognized this, often ending one definition and creating the next with a very different meaning than the one before. Thus I went on to read, "a surface of a thing, be it an object, such as the top of a table, etc. Or, the side of a surface that is marked, such as a clock, playing cards, dominos, etc., or the finished side of fabric, leather, etc." That certainly covered a large and diverse array of things, but still we're very familiar with all of them and don't find it too puzzling. Lots of things to mull over in that definition, but figured I'd better be heading towards home, as we were expecting company in the evening.

Since it was such a beautiful day, I decided to take the long way home and soon rode by the country club and found myself facing the golf course. It sure had lots of hills, sand traps, and water holes, and such beautiful greens. Then I remembered, the "topography of an area" is actually its face. Certainly the topography of this course was interesting and beautiful. It's a good thing I enjoy the scenery, because I've always had trouble connecting "the striking surface of the club" with the golf ball.

Oh no, it's starting to rain, and it's coming down pretty hard. Better slow down a little so I'll be "ready to meet any condition" I may come upon. Looks like the rain is going to continue, so may as well turn around and face home. True, I'll have to face up to the fact that there's work to be done there, but I'll just have to put on a happy face and get it accomplished. Then when our company comes over this evening, I can face them proudly, knowing that I've done well.

Gas [gas]

This day and age, everyone seems to be talking about the price of gas. It's become a commodity that most people find as a necessary item that we continue to buy. Perhaps we can cut down on some driving for leisurely rides, but we still have to drive our cars to work, to appointments, etc., etc.

What is gas? "1. The fluid form of a substance in which it can expand indefinitely and completely fill its container; form that is neither liquid nor solid: vapor; "2. Any mixture of flammable gases used for lighting, heating, or cooking." I'm thankful for those elements every day, whether I'm cooking and baking things in my oven, or just sitting in a nice, warm house curled up and reading a book.

Now Noah takes quite a turn: "3. any gas, as nitrous oxide used as an anesthetic." Having had some surgery, I'm eternally grateful that anesthetics were used. Do we really fill the gas tank of our car with this stuff? Well, not exactly. What we put into our car is *gasoline*, "a volatile, highly flammable, colorless liquid mixture of hydrocarbons produced by the fractional distillation of petroleum and used as a fuel in internal combustion engines."

Well, of course we knew that; we associate it with the price of crude oil, so yes, easy to understand. Then why do we call it gas? Isn't it interesting that we're so fond of this product that we all call it by its nickname just like our best pals.

Now you may find this a real gas to get to the bottom of it all. Yes, *Webster's* reminds us that "it can delight and amuse us greatly" to have this information and pass it on to others. Don't give off so much "idle or boastful talk" that others are offended by it though. They may actually think of you as a gasbag—yes, "one of those people who just talks too much"—become offended. In fact, you can get so tired of listening to such a person that it makes you sick to your stomach. I know what can happen then, and it's a pretty miserable feeling. Yes, "that gaseous substance formed in the stomach and bowels." Whoops, sorry. Now if only that could fill our car's gas tank.

Heart [härt]

There aren't many words in *Webster's Dictionary* where he actually writes so many definitions, which we are all so familiar with, and yet they all contain the fundamental word. First I'll give the basic meaning: "the hollow, muscular organ in a vertebrate animal that receives blood from the veins and pumps it through the arteries by alternate dilation and contraction." Yes, life itself is dependent upon a heart; that's a fact.

We also know that it is used to mean "A. near the center, the central core of a plant or vegetable; B. the innermost part of a place or region, such as the heart of a city."

However, we use this word to cover so many other aspects of emotions and so many human feelings—"love, devotion, sympathy; mood." Probably all of us feel some of these emotions most every day. It's something that makes our heart feel good when we share such feelings.

In February, I have received and sent cards to celebrate St. Valentines Day on the fourteenth. Undoubtedly somewhere on the card was a picture of a heart, "a conventionalized design which is the representation of a heart." To get one sends waves of something special. It might be from someone who stole your heart completely, and what a feeling!

Of course, when you love someone from the bottom of your heart, you know your heart's in the right place, even if your head may be in the clouds. People can tell you that they knew you were in love, as you were wearing your heart on your sleeve. All you knew was that every time you looked at your new love, you felt your heart skip a beat.

At this point, you probably never worried about the fact that when someone stole your heart so quickly and you thought you loved them with all your heart and soul, that this person could have a change of heart, or only love you with half a heart. You could suddenly have your heart broken in just a heartbeat. Then, unfortunately, you open yourself to feeling heartache, "sorrow and grief," such as you have never felt before.

Don't give up though. Take heart. Even when a first love may slip away, set your heart at rest, know that someone else can come along who will produce even greater feelings, ones that you'll find can fill your heart completely. Hopefully then you'll find such happiness that you can live your life to your heart's content, "as much love as you may ever desire," and that you'll find a fairy-tale ending and live happily ever after.

Instrument [ˈinstrəmənt]

It would be interesting to take a poll of a hundred people and find out what was the first thing that came to their minds when they saw this word. Obviously Webster wanted to please every mind when he came up with the definitions for it. Some of them are a bit puzzling to me. First of all, I'll start with the basic Latin word and the interpretation given there. *Instrumenium*: "meaning a tool or tools, stock, furniture, dress." Hmm, really?

Well, now to see how Webster interprets it. "1a. A thing by means of which something is done b. A person used by another to bring something about." Well, a little far-fetched to my way of thinking—certainly not my first thoughts.

"Tool or implement, especially one used for various delicate work or for scientific or artistic purposes."

That's understandable. Look at all of the new instruments used in the medical field. Tiny new surgical tools, especially when it comes to inserting items through veins, laser surgery, and many more modern innovations.

I've actually heard that they think the new generation of doctors may include many who were teenagers glued to their TV sets, playing video games. If they accomplished nothing else, their fingers became so agile that they will adapt to all of these new types of surgery. Scary, but it does make sense. This is also evident in the world of art—paintings, sculpture, all of the artistic areas utilizing new mediums that require new tools. So wonderful.

In this generation, we've come to new meanings that I'm sure Webster could never have imagined, but it does state "various devices for indicating or measuring conditions, performance, position, direction, etc., or sometimes for controlling operations, especially in aircraft or rocket flight." (Obviously we recognize that these definitions were added somewhere along the way. Don't think that Noah really had too much knowledge about some of these items, but I'll still give him credit for the basic ones.) Now these we're all aware of. Every day we see new wonders of how scientists have come up with new instruments for flying airplanes, tracking weather conditions all over the world and even in outer space, finding out what the planets are made of, landing rockets on the moon..

Once again, Webster's turns in yet a different direction—in law: "a formal document, as a deed, contract, etc." Well, having recently purchased a piece of property,

I am completely familiar with those definitions, yet they certainly weren't my first choice.

And then finally came the definition that I had been waiting for: "any of various devices producing musical sound, as a piano, violin, oboe, etc." Guess I have to admit to perhaps a Charlie Brown mentality. The first thing that popped up in my mind was Schroeder playing his piano.

Jam [jam]

I was really hungry this morning and decided to have a piece of toast for breakfast. There is nothing better in the morning than the smell of coffee brewing, hearing the toast pop out of the toaster and scurrying to catch it before it hits the floor. Oh, yes, there is one thing better. Not just plain toast, but with butter and jam. A friend had given me a jar of jam after I had helped her out of a jam. Raspberry, my favorite variety. Fruity, red and sweet, I spread the delectable treat thickly and generously over the buttered toast. Yummy, and the day was jammin' now! Why is jam "jam" and not jelly?

Then I figured I'd better get back to writing. I, of course, had decided on the word for today, but was a bit taken back while reading the first definition. "1. To squeeze or wedge into or through a confined space." Well, that could be a problem if one continued to eat too much of that tasty toast, and I understood that, but gosh that jam was good!

Next, "2. to bruise or crush; b) to force a thumb, toe, etc. back against its joint so as to cause impaction." Think that's another way of loudly saying, "Ow!" Yes, not only have I heard about this, I've experienced it. I'll never forget the time that while trying to open a jar of jam, the jar slipped a bit, causing my hand to fly up and hit the cupboard, jamming my thumb against it so hard that I was afraid I'd actually sprained it. Well, as tears welled up in my eyes, I wiggled my thumb and realized that it did indeed seem to be working in a normal manner. As if that wasn't bad enough, however, I looked at the next jam I'd gotten myself into. When the jar slipped, it had opened, and some wonderful strawberry-rhubarb jam had made quite a mess on the table.

Enough about that. These seem just like the usual familiar type of definitions. How about something a bit different? "6. To wedge or make stick so that it cannot move or work (to jam a rifle)." Maybe the hunters or those who have been or are in the armed forces came up with that one easily. I could equate better to when the cookie press becomes jammed—perhaps not as dangerous as with a rifle, but annoying anyhow. "7. to make (radio broadcasts, radar signals, etc.) unintelligible, as by sending out others on the same wavelength." Now that one never entered my head at all until having read it.

Finally here's one that all of us know, even kids. It's used in the music world: "a jazz session where everyone who wants too can get together and just improvise." Yes, a real jam session as they play along. In fact, it can be so good that we can find "a group of people so close together as to jam a passageway" at the arena where the group is playing and causes problems inside and even traffic jams outside. This can actually produce "a difficult situation; indeed, a real predicament."

Let's see, where did we start all of this? Oh yes, the very last item that Webster mentions in the last sentence of this whole definition: "a food made by boiling fruit with sugar to a thick mixture."

Excuse me; I worked up an appetite. Think I'll have another piece of toast with jam on it.

Kind [kīnd]

It's kind of, "somewhat, rather," a gray day today, so it's been kind of difficult to start writing. I've thought a little about what word to pick out, but there are so many different kinds, "variety," to choose from that I'm having a hard time.

My kind friends, "sympathetic, generous," would probably encourage me if I gave them a call, but that's not really fair. It's also just not my kind of style.

Perhaps today I'd like the word to be something that brings about kind feelings, "friendly, gentle, tenderhearted." Yes, on a day like this, it's good to think of pleasant, lovely thoughts and remember all of the kindly, "a characteristic nature or general disposition marked by such qualities," persons that have been a part of my life. Somehow that brings thoughts of my dad. Not too surprising, as the base of this word for today comes from *kin*.

We had a good relationship, and his kindness, "the state, quality, or habit of being kind," was evident to everyone. He rarely raised his voice; poor Mom had to be the disciplinarian. There wasn't a kindless, "lacking natural feelings," bone in his body. In fact, most people took kindly to, "be naturally attracted to," him, be it at work, in the neighborhood, or in the family. He was such a kind-hearted soul, "having a kind heart, sympathetic," that Mom felt people took advantage of him. Perhaps that was true, but indeed he was my kind of guy. A shining example for me. He was the sort of man that we wish all humankind, "essential characters," might be. What a wonderful world filled with peace that could be. Wed certainly be a one-of-a-kind nation that would be a shining example for all of the world to follow.

Well, perhaps that's too much to hope for, but it's been kind of fun going in all directions—present, past, and projecting ahead. Don't judge me harshly for diverting; so on this one, be kind, "SYN, implies the possession of sympathetic or generous qualities," even if I've rambled on. Please continue on with me with my search for various kinds of words to see what paths I may wander down on the upcoming pages.

Line [līn]

Haven't written in a while, so thought I'd drop you a line, "a short letter, note, or card." It's a beautiful day, and I've been enjoying just looking out the window by my desk. Clean sheets, washed just that morning, are on the clothesline, flapping in the breeze. A smile flits across my face as my glance traces the clotheslines to the old tree the lines are attached to, bringing back memories. There are lines carved into the bark that are still just slightly visible. Our son made them when he was about to carve his initials in it when he got his first jack knife, but Dad stopped him before the deed was completed. Better not go any further along those lines of thinking.

The fisherman out in that boat on the lake is reeling in his line, "a long, fine, strong cord with a hook, sinker, leader, etc. used in fishing." He must have a big fish on the other end. A great day for him. Yeah for the fisherman; poor fish!

Suppose I could have called you on the phone, "a wire or wires connecting stations in a telephone or telegraph system." However, I haven't been feeling top-of-the-line. Therefore, sitting comfortably with a cup of tea next to me and looking out the window while writing seemed much more comforting. Believe it or not, I think I'm making a little progress here. I can change those frown lines on my face into a little happiness; it's starting to take form.

Now I'll relate something that's sure to make me happy and, therefore, is bound to make me feel better. It's our grandson's high school homecoming tonight, and we're going to the game. Yes, I know we'll have to stand in line with lots of other people to get tickets, "a row of persons waiting in turn to buy something," and then line up to go through the gates, but we'll have fun. There's just something special when we see that football field with all of the white lines across it, "a mark made on the ground for certain sports," which will mark the progress of the home team and hopefully lead them to the goal line to score a touch down. Oh, the excitement when they announce the line up for the game and the boys come running out in a line onto the field. The crowd will go wild cheering.

Can hardly wait to see that first line of scrimmage, "the players arranged in a row on either side of the line of scrimmage at the start of each play." It's always fun to see the cheerleaders do their dance line routines and get everyone all cheering the team on to victory. I love it when everyone gets to shouting, "Hold that line!" ("to try to carry the ball through the opposing line"). We hope we'll see the headlines in tomorrow's paper showing a big victory for us. I don't want to feed you a line, "persuasive or flattering talk that is insincere," about how good the team is, but when that front line meets the other team, "a position in closest contact with the enemy during combat," they're awesome.

No matter what line of business, "a person's trade or occupation," the parents of these kids are in, they all want to be out there to see the big game. They really show them great support. It's fun to be a part of it.

Well, just about time to close, the deadline for getting dinner going is near. Oh, by the way, if you are still thinking of coming up for a visit, I heard that the new bus line, "a transportation system between two or more points," —think it's called Travel Trends—has some special rates. Looked it up online, "checking something on the internet," and they looked really good. Tell me when you get the times picked out for the visit so I can line up, "organize efficiently," some fun things to do. I'm sure looking forward to seeing you. Sending you lots of love.

P.S. Just drop me a line when you have things arranged, and I'll take it from there.

Major [mājər]

When we got to be in the higher grades of high school, we had to start some serious thinking about just what our major may be in college, "a field of study in which a student specializes and receives his degree." Of course, we might not always be sure if what we chose would indeed turn out to be the right one, but most of us probably could change our majors along the way if we so pleased. It may mean having to take a few more credits, but it could be worked out.

My husband graduated with a degree in agriculture, which he had chosen as his major in college, but he never did anything more in that field (just a small pun there). Actually, he enjoyed ROTC (Reserve Officers Training Corp) at college and served in the army and after that became a salesman, and that was his major role for many years. He did continue on with Army Reserves and became a major, "an officer above a captain and below a lieutenant colonel," before he retired.

Sure, when we're kids, we have dreams about becoming lots of things. I was sure at the age of twelve that my future would bring me fame as a concert pianist. Thinking back, probably the major, "constituting the majority: said of a part," portion of audiences who heard me play knew that I'd probably not be destined for such a career. I could play pretty well, and at least had been well educated in the field and knew the difference between a major, "designating an imperfect interval greater than the corresponding minor by a semitone," and minor scale.

As I grew older and became a major, "Law. a person who has reached his full legal age," I at least found great enjoyment in my music but had definitely realized that there were other major roles, "Logic: broader; more inclusive," in life and found enjoyment in the roles of wife and mother, hoping that the children would find music to be as important in their lives as it continues to be in my life. However, we know that we can't make any major decisions for our kids; they have to decide for themselves. It was obvious that the boys seemed more interested in watching major league, "principal league in a professional sport," baseball and football on TV rather than practicing music.

By now, I'm positive that the majority, "the greater part of larger number; more than half of a total," of you feel that I've delved into my personal life much more than necessary. My only excuse is that my husband and family are indeed the major loves of my life.

Nod [näd]

Here's a simple word, only three letters, certainly shouldn't be too many ways to go with it, so guess I'll give it a try. First, the simple, basic definition that was quickly thought of: "to shake the head; to move about." But, now Noah goes on, "to bend the head forward slightly and raise it again quickly as a sign of greeting, command, or agreement." Hence the saying we've probably all used when describing some persons we've met as just a nodding acquaintances, meaning not knowing them very well. Hey, I feel like Webster—just making up my own definitions. Enough of that, I'd better get back to following Webster. If not, you may be following the routine of *Webster's* next definition: "to let the head fall forward involuntarily because of drowsiness; be very sleepy." Sometimes *Webster's* does confuse me a bit. If that last motion is involuntary, why does he say to *let it fall forward?* Doesn't involuntary mean that you can't control it?

Perhaps I'm getting lulled into that last definition, meaning I'm starting to get rather drowsy. There must be some place else where this word is used that might be a bit more interesting. Let's go into another realm—that of the outdoor world. It's always so beautiful to look outside when the wind is blowing slightly and see "the tops of trees, flowers, plumes, etc. sway back and forth or up and down," all nodding so beautifully. I think of the beautiful words from the Nutcracker Suite's "Dance of the Flowers." I'm practically humming it now and thinking about the words, "Lilies lilting, tulips tilting, and forget-me-nots remembering."

With that, I believe I have become lulled into taking a nap. You know... slip into the Land of Nod. You've probably felt that way at times also, and what's more pleasant than feeling drowsy and just nodding off? However, if you're not ready to stretch out on the davenport by now, get a volume of *Webster's* out and look up Land of Nod, found in the L section, and you may be in for a big surprise.

Once [wəns]

Once upon a time, "at some time in the past," I met a man who had been through a period in his life when he was almost ready to give up on everything. I knew that he could probably become a success if once given a chance. I only had an opportunity to really talk to him once, "one time only," about how he had strayed away, as he was a bit hesitant to confide in anyone.

He wasn't at a point when he was completely down and out, but I asked him if he would join me for dinner, just once. He did, and what an interesting conversation we had. It turned out that once he'd been living the high life as a top executive in one of our well-known companies. It was, however, getting extremely stressful. His wife knew how he felt but knew any change would have to be his decision.

I told him that once in a while, "now and then," I'd get those same feelings, but when you give the once-over, "a quick comprehensive look or examination," to any situation, you have to take action and know at once, "suddenly," that you are going in the right direction. If you're not sure of the directions, you have to take time to really sort out your thoughts.

We chatted amiably for quite some time, lingering over our cup of coffee, and it was apparent that a weight had been taken off of his shoulders. As we were finally ready to leave, he thanked me and said that once and for all, "finally; decisively, conclusively," his mind was made up and he knew what career he really wanted to pursue and his decision was final.

I felt good about this person and vowed I'd always remember his name and hope that somehow our talk may have made a difference in his life.

It was several years later when I happened to see his name listed in the religious section in our paper. It was amazing to find that he had become a minister. Reading on, I found that once he had become a minister, he had succeeded in having his own church and congregation. I just had to attend his church at least once and did just that the next Sunday and enjoyed the service so much. Truly a once-in-a-lifetime happening to meet this man again. As I left the church and went through the line to shake hands with him, he put his arms around me, gave me a big hug, and called me by name. Then he told me what an impact

I'd had in his life by giving of my time and helping him to make a new start.

We met several times after that, and I was included in many family get-togethers and enjoyed his wife and family. This was, however, not the end of the story. Once we talked and compared family histories, it turned out that he was a cousin once removed, "by one degree or grade." Just goes to prove that what can seem a simple act by one person can have a profound effect on another. It also proves that the once-upon-a-time storybook beginnings can once in a while, "now and then; occasionally," have a truly wonderful storybook ending.

Polydactylism [päli'dakəlēizəm]

Don't actually know anyone personally who fits into this category. It doesn't happen very often. In fact, if someone has this affliction, they may even make the news. Probably just in the local papers, but could even be in some medical papers. Or they may never want anyone to know about it. This is probably found more often in various animals than in humans, and indeed it is an oddity, but in some species, it happens quite often.

I'll dissect the word a bit. First, look at the first four letters: P O L Y. Doing a little research, found that there are 108 words listed in the dictionary that start with those four letters, showing how it was combined with other words. I'll show you a few of them.

Polyrhythm: "the use of strongly contrasting rhythms in simultaneous voice parts."

Polyethylene: "any of several thermoplastic resins."

Polyclinic: "a clinic or hospital for the treatment of various kinds of diseases."

Polyvalent: "designating a vaccine effective against two or more strains of the same species of microorganism."

Okay, here are a couple that most of us do hear about quite a bit this day and age.

Polyunsaturated: "containing more than one double or triple bond in the molecule as certain vegetable and animal fats."

Polygamy: "the state or practice of having two or more husbands or wives at the same time."

Now I'll go back to the first paragraph. As you may suspect, there is a story to relate about this word.

My daughter had an animal that had this condition. She wasn't too perturbed about it, as she admired Ernest Hemingway quite a bit and knew that he had cats who had these traits. He was so fond of his cats that his home, which serves as a museum in Key West, Florida, is filled with cats that are all descendants from the many cats he had as pets while he lived there. Many of them have inherited this same trait.

I heard recently about someone who has a cat who has seven toes on each paw, front and back, so a total of twenty-eight toes. Apparently, about 15 percent of cats are born with extra digits.

It's a condition called *polydactylism.* Yup, there's the word. And, the definition according to *Webster's* is, "having more than the normal number of fingers or toes."

Now this could be rather confusing, or it could be a godsend. Considering that at times we talk about counting up numbers by using our fingers and toes, most of us could only count up to twenty. Having a total of twenty-eight toes could really be an asset.

Quarter [kwôrtər]

Now we'll march on to quarter. I believe that all of you will easily come up with meanings for this word, as we use it practically every day. First the monetary. The majority of people will have a quarter in their purses or pockets. That's easy. "It's a coin that represents one fourth of a dollar." Many of us find that we walk at least a quarter of a mile a day, meaning "one-fourth of a mile." This measurement applies to hours, pounds, years, etc., all referring to one-fourth of any amount.

From here on in, I will merely print them. In football and basketball, it is "any of the four periods in which a game is divided." I do enjoy sports, and especially enjoy watching professional football on TV. I've many times pitched in a quarter when someone has come up with a little wager on some of the big games. Well, probably more than a quarter, as they usually break the bets down to smaller winners in each of the quarters, and then a larger amount after the final quarter, but let's march on.

When thinking about placing bets, horseracing immediately comes to mind. My kids like horses. Certainly don't know how that came about. When getting into close quarters with horses, it's far too close for me. They have, however, persuaded me to attend some racetracks, and there's certainly lots of betting going on by most of the attendees there. Being not very lucky at placing wagers, I'll leave that to others. Have to admit, though, that watching the many quarter horses, "any of a breed of horse developed in America, characterized by a low, compact, muscular body and great sprinting speed for distances up to a quarter of a mile," was awesome, and their strength and stamina are amazing. When I expressed that to my kids, they had a good laugh and informed me that most of the horses were thoroughbreds. I pretended to know what they were talking about, but I don't understand why a quarter horse can't be a thoroughbred too. Obviously I need more education about horses.

Turning now into some other directions, "any district or section in a city." In a city where there are many ethnic areas, often the local people will refer to the Greek district, or the Italian or Polish, etc., districts. Of course, in country real estate you'll often find references such as the NW quarter section of the Eastern section, etc., when describing parcels of land. Nautical, "the after part of a ship's side, between the beam and the stern." Military, "to assign soldiers to lodgings." My husband served in the army both in the U.S. and in Japan. He was a good letter writer and always gave great detailed descriptions about the various quarters he was staying in. Of course I also heard more than once how the blankets on the beds had to be pulled so tight that when a quarter was tossed on it, it had to bounce. Don't think my bed making would follow such tight rules. Finally, "To defile a body by cutting it into quarters." Yuck! Think I'll just end here.

Routine [roō'tēn]

We all can have them! They're free for the making. If you set your alarm to wake you up in the morning you have a routine, "a regular, more or less unvarying procedure." Now the next step is actually getting up. I'm afraid I've gotten into the routine of pushing the snooze button for an extra ten minutes of dozing. So goes the daily routine. We don't have to eat each meal at exactly the same time every day. Of course, your husband and family may expect it and may not appreciate it if dinner is an hour later than usual. At least they are still fed—that's the usual routine, of course.

Now in the business world, everything seems to fit in the same category—the usual routine way to write a letter, the usual routine way in which the telephone is answered. The usual way to dress properly, and following certain protocols at all times. It's the "customary, prescribed, or habitual daily business routine." Of course, any of these things could turn around if the boss so dictates. Oh yes, authority can change routines dramatically, but then, remember, everyone seems to enjoy casual Fridays.

Now that I'm talking business, I realize I've only been discussing the human element. Ever tried to change a routine on a copying machine? That can be pretty messy. Loading eight-by-ten paper to copy legal-sized documents just doesn't seem to work. Neither does pressing ten copies, walking away, and coming back to discover that you pressed one hundred by mistake.

I have to admit to doing each of the above at one time or another. Then there's that dreaded machine, the computer, whose code of operating commands that you follow routines or suffer the consequences. If you meant to push save but push delete instead, it brings about strange sounds—gasps, moaning, suppressed (hopefully) nasty words, sometimes even producing tears, but that just comes from those poor, simple humans who are sitting in front of this awesome machine and think they control it. Yes, there's "a set of coded instructions for a computer," but when we break those routines, it can really seem disastrous.

Let's get out of the office. There are some routines that can never vary. We recently watched a DVD of the 75th Anniversary of the Christmas edition of the Rockettes from Radio City. Couldn't imagine watching a performance of The Rockettes where a couple of the beauties high kick with their left legs when the others are kicking right. No room for error here. They have to follow certain routines exactly, "a series of steps for a dance."

So now as is the usual routine in all essays, they have a beginning, some content, and an end. Now I'll end this one with, may you all enjoy having routines and knowing which should be followed exactly, which can be varied, and which should not and cannot be changed.

Secrets [ˈsēkrit]

In the world of Webster, a secret is defined as "something known only to a certain person or persons and purposely kept from the knowledge of others." I'm almost positive that all of you have shared a secret—either telling it to someone else or having someone tell one to you.

I know I certainly have. Now, here's the tricky part. Why does anyone tell another person a secret? It's probably something that they just have to get off of their chest but don't want everyone to know. However, how do we know for sure that the person we've shared this secret with will never pass the item onto others? Wouldn't feel very happy if before long, twenty people had this information.

I remember only too well the old game of Telephone." Perhaps ten or twelve people would line up in a row, and the lead person would whisper something into the ear of the person standing next to them. This would repeat with all in the line doing the same thing. Then the last person would say out loud what had been told to them. Rarely would it be exactly the same as when the first person had whispered it into the ear of the next person. In fact, it usually was extremely different from when it was first stated. Seems everyone likes to dramatize a bit and add a word here and there. It's possible that what can happen is that in a short time a secret shared from one person to the next, etc. etc., has suddenly changed into that dreaded word: *gossip*!

Now we see the trust that is involved in sharing a secret and feel the burden that we take on when someone says, "I want to share a secret with you." Feel honored, but be ready to carry that burden.

Now's the time when we each must measure our own integrity. Can you hardly wait to share the secret with your other good friend? Or do you wait as long as you can, but finally it just sort of happens to spill out to someone along the way? I remember one time in particular when a secret told to me by a dear friend was held firmly in my head and heart only to hear the same thing repeated by another mutual friend.

If that's the case, I can't help but remember that terrible, but perhaps sort of true, statement, "Telephone, telegraph, tell a woman." Did I just repeat that?

This saying came obviously from the mouth of someone of the male gender. He probably said it to a good male friend, adding, "Don't ever repeat that to my wife or anyone else, for that matter, but I trust you and know that you will keep it just as *our* secret."

Text [tekst]

I finally have a word where I may be ahead of Webster—
at least in the dictionary edition that I've been using.
However, give him a chance.

First, "the actual structure of words in a piece of writing;
wording; 2a. The actual or original words used by an author
b, the exact or original words of a speaker." And, in the same
category, "the principle matter on a printed or written page
as distinguished from notes, headings, illustrations, etc."
In music, "the words of a song." Okay, think he's covered
that quite well, and I understand that when reading a book,
I'm reading the text—got it.

Next, he switches reference specifically to the Bible:
"a biblical passage quoted as authority for a belief or as the
topic of a sermon."

Noah now mentions two words that incorporate this
word *text* along with another specific word that gives it
a new definition. The first is *text hand*, meaning "any of
several black-letter styles of type." The next being *textbook*,

"a book giving instructions in the principles of a subject of study." Of course, this is one that is recognized by everyone, and probably all of us at one time or another have used such books somewhere in our schooling, as usually we had one for every course that we have taken. For those of us who have attended college, we've also found them to be a huge, but necessary, expense we had to pay out to buy one for each course, and bargains on any were seldom found, as they seemed to print up new books every year, so used ones were deemed ineffective. Sorry for the little tirade on that subject, but got it out of my system anyhow.

Now that I've said all of that, I'll venture into the new century. 4 ths I c othr wys 2 msge u. Hello cell phone; good bye "proper English," but perhaps we're just learning a new phonetic language, one that completely ignores any rules we may have learned concerning proper spelling. We are in the world of...*text messaging.*

Ths cn b dwnfal of lrning 4 nxt gnration, & nitmar 4 ritrs &any 1 n prntng ndstry. R u folowg me? I hv 2 thnk 2 rt ths, bt the nxt gnration snd msg so quik my fngrs hrt jst c ing thm zng ovr kybrd. I gt 2 a teen 4 instructs as 2 hw 2 c wht its all abot. Tyvm 4b ing stl with me & 4 giv any mstaks. Im 2 old 4 lrnig new ways!

Whew, I'm back to my dull, hopefully precise way of communicating. I'm having a little laugh for myself right now though. I'm going to finish this and click my little mouse up to spell check and see what happens. This should be fun. Hope I don't knock my computer out of whack.

Unit [ˈyoōnit]

This seems like such a simple, basic word, and that it is. *Webster's* first describes this word in mathematical terms: "(a)the smallest whole number: one," and then goes on to enlarge on that: "(b)a magnitude or number regarded as an undivided whole; (c)the number in the position just to the left of the decimal point." That should certainly cover enough to give full meaning to this word, but then, as Webster seems to do, he goes on to elaborate and give further definitions where this same word may be used. Next, "any fixed quantity, amount, distance measure, etc. used as a standard; specifically a fixed amount of work used as a basis in awarding scholastic credits; usually determined by the amount of hours spent in class."

Now we march into the pharmacy or the doctor's office, and we find another use of this word: "the amount of a drug, vaccine, serum, or antigen needed to produce a given result." This is a very important word to keep in mind every time we have a prescription filled. There have been terrible errors made on occasions where the amounts of units in a prescription can be bungled, and it could produce terrible effects, possibly even death. This word is beginning to sound extremely complex and even dangerous.

Let's jump to the military: "an organized body of troops, airplanes, etc., forming a subdivision of a larger boy."

Noah, at times you really boggle me. Here's a word that is spelled the same, pronounced the same, and sounds the same, but you have managed to come up with definitions that jump rapidly from meaning one to meanings that can jump to thousands and hardly skip a beat in doing so. Obviously my mind just can't seem to jump that dramatically and in just such an abrupt, stern manner. Maybe I'll try and find some pleasant connotations for you and for myself.

Hmm, this seems to be presenting a bit of a problem. Everything just seems to be coming back referring to single or designated quantities. It all seems so cut and dried, not giving any directions to go to show any deviations.

Okay, bear with me; there's a game where you can add one letter and find either another word or change the meaning of the word in question, and I've thought of a letter that does both: unite. Now I'm going to go down the romantic road. We have a man (one unit) and a woman (one unit). They meet, fall in love, and decide to get married. Yes, here it is; one small *e*, and we've these two isolated souls who are each an individual unit and joined them together to once again form a unit that will possibly go on to have children, grandchildren, etc., and so from the joining of these two units, a whole new family unit will be forming, and that could go on to many new additions.

Maybe that's all just a simple transferring of mathematics, going back to the basic definition, but it sounds much more lovely and magical. Okay, Noah, I know you're right, but I hope I'm not entirely wrong.

Volume [ˈvälyəm]

Trying to decide on a word today was difficult, as my husband was listening to the radio, and the volume, "the quantity, strength, or loudness of sound," was up so high that it was hard to concentrate.

I politely, well perhaps a little loudly, but still in a nice manner, asked him to please turn it down. I'd already experienced one of the definitions of my chosen word, but my mind headed more into the book world.

Via history books and epic movies and DVDs, we're probably familiar with the first meaning of this word: "a roll, scroll, hence a book written on a parchment." That brings up for me visions of *The Ten Commandments, Moses,* or some of those other great films. In my mind's eye, I can see them right now unrolling the scroll and proclaiming rules, laws, and various communications. There was something very mystical about it all. Perhaps you, as I, often wondered how long it took someone to write these proclamations, as they were always done by hand using a quill pen, dipping it in an ink well, and writing in an eloquent calligraphy form and only one scroll, which was the original. Never was there a smudge on those scrolls, never a splatter of ink, never a misspelled word. Really a wonderful work of art. We have indeed come a long way, but perhaps lost some of the beauty.

With the advent of printing presses and typewriters, things advanced a great deal. Soon books began to appear, "a collection of written, typewritten, or printed sheets bound together; book of any of the separate books making up a matched set of the complete work.

Thus began the many volumes of history, biographies, etc., that line so many libraries in homes, schools, and public libraries. All there for us to read, learn from, and enjoy. Thank heavens for all of the writers who took the time to fill multiple pages, thus recording so many facts about people and what was happening in the world. Only through their efforts do we have concepts of what life was all about hundreds of years ago.

Soon another form of information began to appear: magazines, "a set of the issues of a periodical in a fixed period of time, usually a year." Not only are they available on shelves in various types of stores, but also many of us may subscribe to several of our special favorites, and they are delivered directly to our homes via mail. What an update and well-informed population of people we may have on the earth at this time. Well, that's the way it was intended. I don't want to evolve into other issues by discussing if that is a valid statement or not. If we get into environmental channels, we may get the argument that all of that excess use of paper can be detrimental, "quantity, bulk, mass, or amount," filling landfills, etc. Yes, we've learned much more about recycling, but it's still a problem that all must learn to handle more carefully. All of that may speak volumes, "to be very expressive or meaningful," about civilization right now, but I just had to include it.

Oh, now I have to ask my husband to please turn up the volume, "fullness of tone," on the radio again. That's one of my favorite songs, and besides, I'm finally finished writing for the day. Time to sit back, enjoy, and just listen for a change.

Whistle [ˈ(h)wisəl]

For many decades, I have really tried to learn to whistle, "to make a clear, shrill sound or note, or a series of these, by forcing breath between the teeth or through a narrow opening made by puckering the lips," with dismal results. I've barely been able to whistle loud enough to call in any of the many dogs which we have had in my lifetime. That's probably because if they were more than fifty feet away from home, I'm sure they couldn't hear me. As my kids can affirm, I can yell a lot louder than I can whistle.

Finally a simple solution was found—I bought a camp-type whistle, "an instrument for making whistling sounds," to wear around my neck to summon both dogs and kids. The worst part is that practically all of my friends can "whistle a happy tune" with seemingly no effort at all. Really hate to admit that I have actually practiced really hard at times to improve my whistling ability.

Now with practice, I've learned to play the piano quite well, but obviously my fingers learn better than my lips have.

Just can't seem to get it. I've even tried sucking in my breath, having read somewhere that some extremely good whistlers use this method, to no avail.

Guess that I'll just fall into the art of appreciating other aspects of this word by enjoying how well it comes across in other ways. The whistling of the leaves through the trees in the summer time. The various birds as they whistle their special tunes to communicate with one another. Oh, the faint sound of a train whistle in the distance, obviously passing some little whistle stop, "a small town at which a train stopped only upon signal," and traveling on again.

Here comes my friend walking down the driveway. Now, you don't know how much I admire her. Somehow she manages to put a couple of fingers up to her mouth, and she can come up with a whistle that would stop that train anywhere along the tracks. I've never discussed this shortcoming of mine with her, as I usually have a whistle-in-the-dark attitude, "to pretend to be confident when faced with danger or defeat," about everything, and simply refuse to ask her for lessons.

Oh well, she's close enough now, so I can just yell, "Hi, come on down!" I'll happily go inside and pour up a couple of glasses of iced tea, and while we wet our whistle, "to take a drink," I'll just sit down with her and relax and talk about anything and everything. Next time while selecting a word, hopefully I'll just give a little whistle and won't let anything get me down.

Xerography [ziˈrägrafē]

This is probably a simple one. Everyone knows what a Xerox machine is, and what it does is xerography, but, of course, we can't just stop there. That would be too easy. I'll first look at *Webster's* most detailed explanation of the word. That, of course, will be followed by my observations. Here's *Webster's* definition: "a process for copying printed material, pictures, etc. in which the latent image of the original material is transferred by the action of light to an electrically charged surface to which the image attracts oppositely charged dry ink particles which are then fused in place on the copy paper, reproducing the original image."

Not only is that an overwhelming definition, the whole concept boggles my mind. I may now, however possibly understand the function of toner! It even makes me want to do a little more research as to how this machine was invented and who really invented it. The truly amazing thing is that most everyone knows how to use this machine.

Many of us even have one in our home, and I doubt that most companies would contemplate being without one. It's just taken for granted, as if it's always been around.

In the present time, it seems like a necessity. Why? Well, first of all, in the business world, it seems that every piece of paper that is written, has to have at least six copies readily available. Back when I worked in an office, all of the papers were typed (old-fashioned word and done on an old-fashioned machine; a typewriter. Now it's on the word processor or on the computers). Thank heavens the Xerox machine not only prints, but also collates up to hundreds of pages in nothing flat.

Let me tell you about the old days while working in any office. The good secretary typed up every report, very often using up to ten sheets of typing paper with a piece of carbon paper in between each of them. There weren't even electric typewriters available, and you had to have strength enough in your fingers to pound the letters hard enough to make sure that the impression would go through all of those carbons and sheets of paper.

Now in those days, there was no spell check or simple delete and respelling of anything. An accurate typist was well respected, as everyone knew that if an error was made, it had to be corrected—first by coating the error with correction fluid, or, in later days, a piece of correcting tape, and then typed over. It didn't just stop there, however, because each of those carbon copies also had to be corrected, and that was a really messy procedure.

All right, I won't go any further. Just remember, any of you who utilize this wonderful Xerox machine should approach it with respect, treat it gently, and say thank you when you gather up the copies in your hands. Oh yes, every time you use one, pray that it doesn't break down. P.S. try saying this word without pronouncing the *X* as a Z.

Yawn [yôn]

This is a simple word and really doesn't need much explanation, but it's also a fun one to think about.

Webster's starts this one with "to open the mouth wide, esp. involuntarily, and with a deep inhalation, as a result of fatigue, drowsiness or boredom." Yes, there is one more meaning—sort of the same, but sort of different: "to be or become wide open; gape; to express or utter with a yawn."

Most people have experienced how really hard it is to suppress a yawn. Sometimes it can happen at a most inconvenient or even embarrassing moment. I find it can happen to me most easily when someone is going into great detail explaining something that I'm not exceedingly interested in. Of course it somehow seems to happen to me when I'm with other people in a large audience.

I distinctively remember an episode when at the university, attending a lecture in microbiology, not exactly my favorite subject. I was trying to pretend being avidly interested in the subject, but started to yawn. At first it was just tiny yawns that were probably not even noticeable to others—I could keep my mouth closed, or simply put my hand up to my mouth and hope that the people next to me never even noticed. Oh, if only they would have at least dimmed the lights in the auditorium. Well, come to think about it, if that had been the case, I probably would have fallen sound asleep. But no, the size of the yawns just increased and simply wouldn't stop. I was getting pretty paranoid now, believing I was probably the only person who wasn't interested in every word that the professor was saying.

As my yawns got bigger, I noticed that a fellow sitting down in the next row looked back at me. It was most interesting to see that his response was to open his mouth and give a big yawn. As he yawned, the fellow next to him yawned also. When I saw that, it made me yawn even more, and that seemed to start a chain reaction up and down the rows. Amazing.

Thankfully, I believe that the professor noticed also, as he abruptly suggested that we take a breather and stand up and stretch for a moment or two. I've also been a victim of the power of suggestion. I've not been sleepy, or bored, but suddenly I've seen one or two other people yawn, and it becomes something that one just has to do, and I find myself yawning also.

It's interesting that Webster uses a word in his explanation that doesn't seem completely true. He states yawning to be involuntary. Relaxation experts at times suggest that a yawn is relaxing, and they suggest that you make yourself yawn. Now this yawn is turned into a voluntary action. It's easy to do. Only problem is that when you open your mouth to do this, you actually *do* find yourself yawning with your mouth wide open, and you don't even know why. Have to admit it is most relaxing anyhow.

This one can be a little game. While sitting amongst a group of friends, or enemies, whatever, and no matter what is going on, start to yawn a few times. Now, take notice of how many others may do the same thing. In fact, I'm yawning just thinking about it. Don't know why this act is so contagious. If only we could get people to smile so easily. Frowns are contagious enough; we don't want to pursue that train of thought. At any rate, it's sort of a fun thing to try.

I don't want to bore you, and certainly don't want you to start yawning. Just turn the page, and perhaps I'll have another word that may spark your interest a bit more.

Zip [zip]

Webster's first definition certainly wasn't my first thought, but here it is: "hissing or whizzing sound, as of a passing bullet." Granted, fortunately I haven't heard too many bullets passing by me, so I'll try the next definition: "energy; vigor, vim." Now that one fits the bill a bit better. I've heard a lot of people talk about themselves or someone else who is full of zip and understand that they are talking about someone full of energy.

Now when you go for the slang meaning, it states, "a score of zero." That dreaded thought we might all have about taking a test and failing miserably, getting a zero. Finally we come to the meaning that I thought of first. When it's time to be going somewhere, you put on your jacket and zip it up. Simple, well, almost. The actual definition for this is *"the act* of becoming fastened or unfastened by means of a zipper." Okay, Noah, think I got the idea.

There is, however, a list of words related to this one. *Zipper:* "a device to use to fasten and unfasten two edges of material: it consists of interlocking tabs which are joined or separated by sliding a part up or down." We already covered the fact that as far as Webster is concerned, this is actually a "person or thing that zips." Now this is a dual purpose that I really have to think about.

Yes, we must have the object (zipper) that is mentioned. Now this can get a little technical, but we need a person to activate this object. This can confusing.

Okay, this person can passively sit and zip up a coat, but a thing that zips by in my thoughts has to be moving quite rapidly, like a speeding car that zips by or a child who zips up the stairs. Oh, this could just go on and on. I somehow never thought that zipping up a jacket could become such a complex thing. Thought I'd just zip on through that part, but I'll just turn in another direction.

Now I've found another of the words derived from the original one, *zippy*, which we have already covered, "full of vim and energy." Yes, I've found a little more zip now, so I'm back on track, and ready to zip ahead. There are two more words that possibly represent different generations, so some of you may possibly never even heard about this one. A *zip gun*: "a crude, improvised pistol, usually consisting of a piece of pipe attached to a wooden stock with a firing pin actuated by a rubber band or a spring." Not exactly what most hunters took with them to try and get pheasants or even squirrels, but little boys seemed to think that it was fun just to try. I've seen a zip gun but never thought they looked like something that I just had to have.

Finally, *zip code*. "a system devised to speed mail deliveries, under which the post office assigns a code number to individual areas and places." This is something that older folks didn't know anything about when they were young, but young people nowadays deem zip codes to be extremely important, and mail simply cannot be sent without using the right numbers, or the sender would probably have the letter returned to them.

Unfortunately I have run into that situation, and I'm not exactly sure where a couple of pieces of my mail have journeyed to before they came back to me. Then of course it took another letter to the same person, enclosing the original piece of mail, but then explaining why it took so long for me to write to them, and admitting that it was my fault for not checking the zip code. I wrote it down more carefully before sending it off again. Obviously a word added on recently into *Webster's Dictionary*.

Now we come down to wondering how someone came up with the term in the first place. I'll just use a bit of imagination, but follow Noah's thinking. *Code* is "information processing in which letters, figures, etc. are arbitrarily given certain meanings" Of course these being the numbers involved to indicate the right sending areas. That makes sense. This chore must have taken a mathematician to figure out and set up. Next, zip means it moves fast. The whole object of the process, of course. This part must have been suggested by citizens wishing to get their mail sent faster and who probably kept telling the mathematicians to get a little more zip to make their brains move faster so that they could get the plan implemented. Finally joining in wedded bliss the combination of the two words: *zip code*.

At any rate, be sure to respect the rules of the post office if you want your mail to arrive as quickly as possible.

Don't ever forget to write in the proper numbers. Now, as happens in *The Twilight Zone*, we have entered the world of the zip code.